Guide for Authors

Guide for Authors

BASIL BLACKWELL

© Basil Blackwell Publisher Ltd 1985

First published 1985

Basil Blackwell Publisher Ltd
108 Cowley Road, Oxford OX4 1JF, UK

Basil Blackwell Inc.
432 Park Avenue South, Suite 1505,
New York, NY 10016, USA

British Library Cataloguing in Publication Data

Guide for authors.
  1. Manuscript preparation (Authorship)
  808'.02   PN160

  ISBN 0-631-13707-6

Typeset by Katerprint Co Ltd, Cowley, Oxford
Printed in Great Britain
by Whitstable Litho Ltd, Kent

Contents

Preface   vii

PART I   **Finding a Publisher**

Which publisher?   1
Making the approach   3
Assessing the response   6
Literary agents   7
Commissioned books   9
General 'trade' books   9
University and scholarly books   10
Books for schools   12
Novels   13
Short stories   14
Poetry   15
Plays   15
Children's books   16
The contract   16

PART II   **Preparing the Typescript and Illustrations**

General presentation   21
Word-processors   22
Pre-delivery checks   22
Headings   23
Preferred styles   24
Quotations   27
Notes   29
Reference systems   30
Tables   35
Lists   36
Special symbols and equations   36
Figures and maps   38
Photographs   39
Copyright permissions   40
Series   42
Edited volumes   43

Translations 44
New editions 44

PART III **Copy-editing, Proofs and Index**

Copy-editing 45
Proofs 45
Indexing 49

Supplementary reading 52

Appendix 1: Providing your text
on a floppy disk 54

Preface

This guide has two purposes. One is to attempt to describe in a small space what an author needs to know in order to find a publisher, prepare a typescript efficiently, and see it through its proofing stages until it emerges as a book. The other is to provide authors under contract with Basil Blackwell with all they need to know about the company's preferred styles and normal procedures.

The two purposes are remarkably complementary. Although Blackwell authors will probably turn first to parts II and III, they may find that the advice in part I on how to present a proposal to a publisher, what to bear in mind when writing a textbook, or what terms to expect in a contract will prove useful when they are thinking about the next book. Equally, questions of style, choice between reference systems and methods of indexing, all discussed in parts II and III, are problems that any author has to tackle, and many of the solutions suggested here are likely to prove acceptable to whichever publisher you choose.

PART I

Finding a Publisher

You want to find a publishing company which will not only accept your book, but will publish it effectively. Effective publication means good editing, design, printing, marketing and promotion: in other words, making all those who might be interested in your book aware of it, convincing them they ought to buy it, and then helping them to do so by ensuring its availability at a price they can afford.

Which publisher?

Your most crucial contact will be your editor: to a large extent, your search for a publisher is in effect a search for an editor. The editor (also called 'publisher', 'commissioning editor', 'sponsoring editor', 'editorial director', etc.) is the person who will accept your book, and who will take final responsibility for its success or failure. He or she will also advise you about its content, structure and level, will encourage you when you're stuck, share your enthusiasm when the book is finished, and in general act as your primary link to the other people in the company who will help to produce and publish it successfully. Finally, once your book has been published, it will be the editor who discusses the next one with you. Authors and editors have an identity of purpose: they need each other to survive.

Most editors are under considerable pressure to produce books and to do so profitably. This inevitably means that authors with a good track record are likely to claim more attention than those publishing their first book (even though they may need it more). Do not therefore be hurt if the task of reading your typescript in detail is delegated. The more successful your editor is the more likely he or she is to be sitting in an igloo of typescripts and proposals, both accepted and awaiting consideration. A team of people inside and outside the company will often be called upon for advice and specialist skills. Just remember that, if the treatment you receive is insensitive or inadequate, you can, and should, complain to your editor.

Good publishers nearly always have good editors, and finding the former will usually lead to the latter. By asking friends and colleagues you may be able to go to an editor direct. Otherwise, you would do well to inspect the shelves of your local library and of a good bookseller, noting the publishers of what seem to you to be the best (fairly recent) books in your field. Also keep an eye on the book review pages in the Sunday and daily newspapers (usually the Thursday edition). You should certainly buy a copy of the latest *Writers' and Artists' Yearbook* or (for the United States) the *Literary Market Place*. (For details see the section on supplementary reading below.) The *Writers' and Artists' Yearbook* provides succinct information on every major aspect of publishing (including, e.g., copyright, broadcasting, libel and income tax); the *Literary Market Place* is really meant for publishers and others in the book trade. Both books will tell you who publishes what and where. All publishers specialize in one or more fields and you will save yourself a great deal of postage and frustration if you can match in advance the interests of your potential publisher with your book. This sounds painfully obvious, but you would be surprised how many novels we are offered even though we have never published adult fiction.

What all this means, then, is that, just as the publisher will, you hope, evaluate your book with care and attention, so should you assess the qualities and characteristics of the publisher you approach. Here is a brief checklist of points to consider:

1 Does the company publish in my field? Does it attract good authors?
2 Do its books look good? Are they produced well and priced competitively?
3 Is the company reputable and efficient?
4 Is it international? Does it have a good system of agents throughout the world?
5 Will it offer the kind of editorial and marketing expertise my book requires?

Finding answers to questions 3, 4 and 5 could be difficult. Your bookseller may be able to help on question 3; and you can get some indication of the extent of a company's international operations by looking at the addresses of agents and overseas subsidiaries that are usually printed on the back of the publisher's seasonal catalogues. If you are reasonably confident about 2, 3 and 4, then you can probably take 5 for granted.

Making the approach

This section offers advice on how to approach a publisher with a proposal for a non-fiction book. The fiction section below discusses the rather different task of finding a publisher for a novel. Presenting a proposal is an art, not unlike applying for a job. What you are doing is selling your idea and your ability to carry it out successfully.

When you have drawn up a shortlist of the most appealing and appropriate publishers for your book, you should write to one of them. Unless you have been able to make a personal contact, your letter should be addressed to the editor in your field: for example, 'The Editor: Secondary School Books', 'The History Editor', 'The Philosophy Editor', etc.

It is not usually necessary to have written the whole book before you approach a publisher. Indeed it is quite often better to draft an overall plan, write a couple of chapters, and then get an editor interested. He or she will be able to help you to shape the book to the market, strike the right language level, write to the best length to ensure that it is competitively priced, etc. Even if you have completed the typescript, you should not send it to the publisher until you have been asked to do so. The aim is to tempt the editor to ask to see it, or to see sample chapters.

The proposal

The proposal should consist of a single-sided, typed introductory letter, together with details about the book and its potential readers, and details about yourself. The complete package should not amount to more than five or six pages.

All the information you send should be as concise and as pointed as you can make it. It should be typed and laid out clearly. Depending on the kind of book you are offering, you might provide:

1 A summary (200–300 words) of the book's scope and content, showing the originality of your approach.

2 A (realistic) assessment of who is going to read the book and, not always the same thing, who will buy it. Is it pitched at a particular level of competence? Is its appeal confined to one country or international? You should try to be specific about this: stress the major, not the fringe markets. Suppose, for example, you have written up your research on the long-term effects of chemical fertilizers in domestic gardens. One of your findings is that bonemeal causes cancer of the fingernails. This will have some publicity value, but the major market for the book will be horticultural societies and the fertilizer industry, with fringe markets among environmentalists and cancer researchers. The fact that everyone who has a garden will be interested in your book's conclusions will not be directly related to its success. They will not buy it. Nor will manicurists.

3 A paragraph about the book's relationship to existing works and, if there is competition, why your book is better and more suited to the needs of its potential readers. Say what the competing books are, when they were published, by whom, and at what price.

4 An outline of the contents, with a sentence or two describing each chapter. This will show the book's development and structure. It does not, of course, have to be rigidly adhered to in the final version.

5 A paragraph saying exactly what stage you have reached in preparing the typescript (e.g. two chapters completed and three more drafted), how long the final typescript is likely to be (to the nearest 5,000 words), what number and kind of illustrations it will require (photographs, diagrams, maps, tables, etc.),

4

and whether the book would benefit from being printed in two or more colours. You should admit to any unusual typographical requirements, e.g. phonetic script or Chinese characters.

6 Brief details of your experience and relevant qualifications (preferably on a single sheet of paper). You should list previous major publications, with dates and publishers.

Our late founder and president, Sir Basil Blackwell, used to say that, in considering a book for publication, an editor should ask two questions: 'Will the world be the richer for its publication? And will I be the poorer?' The aim of your initial proposal is to prompt a tentative 'yes' (at least) to the first, and a firm 'no' to the second.

Multiple submissions

It is nearly always best to approach one publisher at a time, but if you are submitting a proposal to two or more you should say so. Considering a book for publication is an expensive and time-consuming business, and you may cause bad feeling which will not be in your long-term interest, if you ask several editors to duplicate each other's work simultaneously. There is a fair chance too, if you try to conceal it, that one of the editors will find you out, and this may result in a rejection you might not otherwise have had.

Return postage

If you are so confident (or unwise) as to send the typescript of your book to a publisher before being asked to, you should include stamps or a money order to cover return postage. But this is, of course, an admission of lack of confidence. The best way to avoid that and the expense is to wait until you have been asked to send your typescript. You may then assume (unless told to the contrary) that there is no need to provide return postage.

Top copies

The question of which copy to send when the time comes is tricky. You should never send a publisher (or a literary agent, or indeed anyone) any proposal, sample

5

chapters or typescript of which you have not retained a fully corrected copy. You should probably keep your top copy until the book has been accepted and you deliver it as the final typescript from which the typesetter will work. A top copy which has been submitted to several publishers will begin to show the signs of a much-rejected book, an impression to avoid at all costs. The answer is probably to make a really good quality photocopy (which should last for several submissions before becoming tacky), or to use a word-processor capable of churning out top copies on demand.

Assessing the response

The initial approach may itself bring an offer of publication and therefore a contract (see below). However, the response, if positive at all, is much more likely to be a request to see sample chapters, or the complete typescript if it is available.

The editor will then set about assessing the quality of the book in terms of writing and content, and will try to establish how many people might buy it. An important consideration here will be the price, which tends to vary directly with the cost of production, and inversely with the number of copies printed. The editor will, in consultation with the sales or marketing department, try to establish the ideal price for the book. If the proposed length of your book pushes the price beyond this level, then you may be asked to cut; should the editor feel that you are not offering the reader value for money, then you may be asked to expand one or more sections.

The editor may also take soundings from experts in your field, overseas branches or agents, and the rights department. You might at this stage begin to feel reasonably encouraged: most editors will try not to consider any book seriously unless they feel there is a good chance of acceptance.

The investigation of the quality and sales potential of your book will take some time, and you may have to be reasonably patient. However, if after three months you have heard nothing, you should write for news, and after six give warning that you plan to take your book elsewhere.

Most publishers reject at least 90 per cent of all the typescripts and proposals offered to them. You should not therefore be surprised if this happens to yours; nor should you necessarily be downhearted. There are many reasons why a typescript or proposal may be rejected which have little to do with its quality. The publisher may have so many books on hand that all funds available for publishing new ones have been exhausted, or may have another book in preparation which is either similar to yours or competes with it. If you are told that your work is unsuited to the list, then you have chosen the wrong kind of publisher.

The rejection letter may describe the book as uneconomic: in other words the editor thinks it could not be produced at the right price, has too few potential buyers, or covers a subject already adequately catered for by existing books. Some criticism or suggestions for improvement may be included, but you should not try to enter into a detailed correspondence with the editor following a rejection. There is little or no likelihood of reprieve.

Try another publisher instead. There may still be hope even after two or three rejections. At that stage, however, it is often best to set the work aside for a while, and then look at it afresh, do some more research perhaps, and consider recasting it. Few authors, even the most successful, have never had a book turned down. Nor are editors infallible: most will have rejected a book that subsequently became a best-seller.

If you have a literary agent then he or she will make the initial approach to the publisher for you. Agents and publishers maintain a respectful distance: the former on the grounds that they are the author's true representatives; the latter on much the same grounds. Publishers exist by virtue of the money they make by exploiting the efforts of their authors. So do literary agents: usually 10 per cent of all earnings in the UK and, where the

Literary agents

agent retains these rights, between 15 and 25 per cent of earnings from overseas English and foreign language publishers.

It is at least as hard to find a good agent as a good publisher, and you should conduct the search for an agent in much the same way as the search for a publisher.

Literary agents frequently specialize, so before writing a preliminary letter you should check in the *Writers' and Artists' Yearbook* to ensure that the agent deals with your kind of book. If you expect your earnings from writing to average less than about £1,000 a year, you are unlikely to be a viable client for an agent. On the other hand, if you plan to earn a substantial part of your income from writing, then an agent can be useful. An effective agent will know the interests and preferences of particular editors, and will match these with your book. · The agent will negotiate the contract on your behalf, probably (depending on the publisher concerned) retaining certain rights to sell separately, usually film, dramatic, broadcasting and serialization, and frequently translation and American rights. If you have an agent you should never discuss financial matters directly with the publisher.

Authors of fiction or general non-fiction are much more likely to have, and to need, agents than authors of university or school books. An agent is almost certainly essential if you derive your income from a mixture of, say, writing books, journalism and broadcasting. The larger agencies employ specialist staff for the different media: they will be aware of opportunities for you to exploit your talents, and they will know (as you may not) the going rates for particular kinds of work.

In many respects, a good literary agent should act like a good editor (and a good editor like an agent): both are concerned to enhance your reputation and your income. But you would be wise not to expect too much at first: telephoning every two weeks, for example, to ask whether your typescript has been accepted is not likely to make you a favoured client. As your income and reputation grow, however, you should expect (and demand) attention, care and inspiration both from your agent and from the publishing house he or she chooses for you.

Although it is possible to find a publisher by submitting an unsolicited proposal along the lines suggested above, in practice most non-fiction books published result from an editor approaching an author, rather than the other way round. An editor will identify a need or demand for a book. Then, if you are well known in the relevant field, he or she may write to you to ask what you think of the idea, and whether you are prepared to put forward a proposal showing how you would write the book.

Commissioned books

Such a proposal should take much the same form as an unsolicited one. However, as the boot is now to some extent on the other (i.e. your) foot, you would be entitled to ask for a draft contract, or at least for a summary of the terms offered. If preparing the detailed outline requires some research, or if you have been asked for one or more sample chapters, then you can reasonably ask for a fee, to be paid at once or on submission of the outline and/or sample chapters. Such fees are normally considered part of the advance on royalties (see the section on contracts below) if the project goes ahead, but are not returnable if it does not.

A large proportion of the books, especially of the hardback books, stocked by the average bookseller will fall into the category that publishers call 'trade' books. These are written for a wide adult readership on any number of subjects from cookery and gardening to psychology and astronomy.

General 'trade' books

Despite the apparently saturated market, there is always room for a new book if it presents a different approach or incorporates new developments. Many are, of course, specially commissioned, but it is possible to find a publisher (or literary agent) by submitting a proposal, followed by sample chapters, in the way described above. Since relatively large print-runs and therefore reasonable prices are particularly important here, you will need to be prepared to work closely with the editor and his or her advisers in tailoring the book to the market.

University and scholarly books

Monographs

Scholarly and research monographs are written to advance the state of knowledge in a particular (often a very particular) subject. Originality and scholarship, both of the research and in the approach or method adopted, are at a premium. These books are published by the university presses and, when the market is large enough to support commercial publication, by independent academic publishers.

Scholarly books are usually restricted in their appeal, but this is not always the case: there is no absolute distinction between such books and those written for the more general market. This is especially so in the humanities (e.g. history and literature) where good writing and the avoidance of jargon can transform the sales potential of a book without compromising its scholarship.

Doctoral dissertations, on which scholarly monographs are sometimes based, are almost never publishable (even by a university press) without substantial rewriting.

First-year textbooks

All introductory textbooks date as the disciplines that they cover advance and change, some (notably in the sciences) faster than others. This means the books must either be updated frequently or replaced. Even the best-established university-level textbook is vulnerable to competition. Whereas in schools cash restraints may hold back the replacement of an outmoded book, university students are expected to buy their own books, so each new intake provides a new potential market.

The essential qualities of a textbook are clarity, objectivity, appropriate pace, balance between explanation and exemplification, and readability. You should try, if you can, to convey to the student some of the enthusiasm you feel about your subject. It may be helpful to remember that a successful textbook can be widely influential in the shaping of a discipline.

You should contact a publisher at an early stage with a detailed proposal. Your editor will almost certainly ask you for one or two sample chapters before giving you a commitment, so have these ready. The proposal and the chapters will be sent to several potential users for detailed comment. After your book has been contracted the editor may well ask you to submit the typescript in sections, so that it can be tested as you write it. Textbook publishing is very much a collaboration between author and editor. Indeed, if your editor does not provide you with any market research or feedback, you should begin to wonder whether you have chosen the right firm.

High-level textbooks

These hover somewhere between introductory textbooks and monographs. Often such a book will have been published first as a hardback. If it makes a substantial impact on its subject in this form, the publisher may think it worthwhile to issue the book as a paperback in the hope that it will be recommended to, and sometimes bought by, students.

If you are setting out with the idea of writing a post-introductory textbook, then you should approach a publisher at an early stage to discover whether a market exists for what you have in mind. Books at this level will sometimes create their own market, for example, in making new theories or discoveries accessible to students.

Edited volumes

A good many books consist of reprinted articles (readings on a particular theme or the works of a particular scholar), or of previously unpublished work (specially written for the volume or revised versions of conference papers). The most viable of these alternatives today is probably the volume of specially commissioned essays, prepared under tight editorial control. For example, in a rapidly changing field a team of people specializing in different aspects can put together a stimulating and authoritative guide to developments. If you decide you want to edit such a volume, then this is one way of setting about it:

1 Sound out your chosen contributors by sending them a description of the book as you see it, with a draft table of contents and a provisional timetable.
2 Ask each person to produce a page or so describing how they would tackle the subject you have in mind for them.
3 If the response from your contributors is positive, revise the proposal accordingly, and send it to the publisher of your choice, together with the one-page summaries and timetable.

Your aim should be to make the book as coherent as possible. You should circulate the chapter summaries to everyone so that each contributor knows what the others are working on. If possible, you should arrange a meeting of contributors before serious writing begins. On the coordination of style, level and references, see the section on edited volumes in part II below.

You will have to be prepared to be tough, to ensure both evenness of quality and adherence to the deadline: one very late contributor can destroy the book's topicality, and lose you friends, if not the contract.

Books for schools

Books used in schools are nearly always written by teachers or by people with teaching experience. They tend to be 'market-specific': this means that they are precisely tailored to particular (often examination) syllabuses, to one level and to a fairly narrow age group. Making early contact with an editor is vital. You should send in a proposal along the lines described above, defining the market as closely as you can. The editor, if interested, is likely to ask you for a short sample section to make sure that you are capable of writing at the level of difficulty and for the age group you have in mind, so you should have this ready before making an approach.

Writing for a syllabus (or part of it) may often be a necessary but is certainly not a sufficient condition for success. The examination boards cater for a wide range of interests and teaching approaches within each subject, and what may seem to be an obvious gap in the available literature may simply reflect the fact that very few people teach that part of the syllabus. You may have a greater chance of success with a new approach to an area already well supplied with textbooks. Before accepting your proposal the editor will investigate whether schools would welcome the book, how widely the subject is taught, and how much time is given to it. The last point is particularly important in judging what should be its ideal length.

If your book is accepted before it is complete, then you will probably find that the contract requires the content, level and approach to be suitable for its market. You may well find, too, that the editor will seek further advice on the completed typescript, which will almost certainly produce further recommendations for modification.

Illustrations are often an important part of a school book, and you will be asked to supply as many suggestions as you can. The publisher will normally assign a freelance artist to do the drawings and will ask you to check them for accuracy and appropriateness of detail. The whole exercise of producing a school book involves close and constant collaboration between author, editor, artist and designer. It can be time-consuming and costly, but the effort may be well rewarded as a successful school textbook can have a very long life.

Novels

Unless you are already an established novelist, there is no point in contacting a publisher or literary agent before a novel is completed to your own satisfaction. Just as most non-fiction books are commissioned, most fiction comes to the publisher from an agent – but it is no easier to find an agent than a publisher. The *Writers' and Artists' Yearbook* lists agents as well as publishers and briefly outlines their special interests and requirements.

It is also worth looking in bookshops and noting down the names of hardback publishers of the kind of work you have written. As with non-fiction, it is best to apply to one firm at a time.

Most agents and publishers prefer you to send a preliminary letter rather than simply to send your typescript. That letter is crucial: it must catch their interest, show you can write well, describe your work so that it sounds interesting, and give any relevant details about yourself. Type the letter neatly, on two pages at most. If your novel can be categorized as detective, thriller, historical, romantic, science fiction, fantasy, etc., then say so. If you have shown your work to an established novelist or critic, it may be worth asking them to write separately in support, or perhaps enclosing a copy of a letter sent to you. If the agent or publisher does then ask to see the typescript, you should always send return postage.

Some literary agents charge a fee (usually between £20 and £30) for considering a first novel. (The *Writers' and Artists' Yearbook* will tell you which do not.) If you are an unpublished novelist, paying this fee may be a good way of getting a reasoned, objective appraisal of your work. Since publishers do not charge authors a fee to consider their books, but at the same time (and possibly for that reason) may simply refuse to consider novels sent to them unsolicited, it may be worth your while to fork out the sum required.

If you do find a literary agent who will take you as a client, you will still need to be patient as it may take some months to place your work with a publisher.

Short stories Volumes of short stories are notoriously difficult to place. Even a best-selling novelist will not as a rule please his or her publisher by offering a collection of short stories rather than a novel. Unpublished authors will stand no chance of success unless and until the fashion in reading changes. At present, the commercial demand for books of short stories is confined almost exclusively to supernatural or science-fiction anthologies. It is much better to submit short stories separately to a magazine or newspaper (some of which run annual competitions for new authors). It may also be possible to get one broadcast on the radio.

Poetry

There are signs of a renaissance in the reading and publishing of poetry. Even so, the market remains small, and few poets or publishers make much money from it. As with short stories, the first step is to publish your poems singly in journals and magazines (of which there are a number devoted specifically to poetry). Only when you have published enough to collect together in a small book should you submit them to a publisher. The best way then is to send photocopies of the printed versions to show that they have appeared, but you should always include a few which have not been published.

Aspiring poets are particularly likely to be asked to 'contribute' to (and in fact to pay for) the cost of producing their own books. Such 'vanity publishing' will do nothing for your reputation which is far more likely to be enhanced by the appearance of your work in a cyclostyled broadsheet – especially one that puts you in company with one or two more established poets. If you really want to see your work in print, then you could consider approaching a local printer and publishing a limited edition yourself. You should send copies out for review to the poetry magazines and advertise through their small ad. sections.

Plays

Plays are written for performance rather than for publication, though they are frequently published after or during a successful run, or if the playwright is already well known. Performing rights in plays are sometimes handled by the publisher of the play, rarely by the playwright, usually by his or her agent.

Once your play has been written it is fully protected

by UK copyright law, but the Society of Authors advises that you should deposit a copy with your bank and obtain a receipt in order to be able to prove the date of completion. Guidance on how to get your play performed (which is similar in some respects to placing a book with a publisher) is given in the *Writers' and Artists' Yearbook*.

Children's books

The process of publishing fiction and non-fiction for older children does not differ in any significant way from that relating to the adult equivalents. Writing for younger children is a more specialist activity, and particular attention needs to be paid, for example, to vocabulary. Nearly all books for younger children are illustrated, sometimes by the author, more usually by a professional illustrator. Most publishers of children's books will have a team of freelance artists and will try to assign to your book an artist appropriate to your style. You should certainly ask to see examples of the artist's work; most publishers will show them to you automatically. If you are already teamed up with an artist, send examples of his or her work when asked to do so, taking care to pack them carefully and to send them by registered post. Even better, make an appointment and carry them to the publisher's office yourself.

The contract

When your book has been accepted for publication, you (or your agent) will receive a draft contract, nearly always called a 'memorandum of agreement'. This will include details of the book's length and illustrations, etc. (which you will already have discussed with the editor) and of how your income from its publication will be calculated. The contract will be signed by you and by your publisher and will thereafter define your formal relationship. Although the contract may arrive on a pre-printed form, the terms are normally negotiable within reason. It is vital for both parties to make sure the contract covers fairly and properly every major aspect of your book's publication and subsequent life.

Read the contract carefully, and ask your publisher to explain in writing anything that you do not understand. Even if you have an agent it is sensible to make sure you understand the arrangements fully. Terms vary considerably from publisher to publisher, and according to the kind of book in question, but the following guidelines are worth bearing in mind.

Where the book is all your own work, you should not part with the copyright. Where you are the editor of a collection of articles or of a reference book, you may be able to retain copyright in some aspect (e.g. editorial organization or structure), but it is often simplest if the publisher takes copyright for this kind of book.

Copyright

Ensure that there is a clause to the effect that, if the book goes out of print or the company goes into involuntary liquidation, all rights revert to you.

Reversion

Make sure that the requirements on length and timing are realistic, and that it is clear who is responsible for obtaining, preparing and paying for the illustrations. If you find subsequently that you cannot meet the deadline for completion, let your editor know well in advance and negotiate a new one (in writing).

Length, illustrations and completion date

As well as checking who is responsible for the illustrations, you need to make sure you are aware of whether you or the publisher will seek permission to reprint copyright material, read proofs, prepare the index, etc. (see also the sections on these topics below).

Permission fees, proofs and index

The contract will usually state that these areas are your publisher's sole responsibility. You go to a publisher for precisely this expertise, so you should be able (if you have chosen wisely) to rely on the publisher's judgement. At the same time most publishers will share design decisions with the author when asked to do so,

Design, pricing and promotion

and all will welcome, indeed may require, your assistance in publicity and promotion. If you feel strongly that your book's success depends on its appearance, then you may want to ask for the formal right to approve the design of the page and of the jacket. If so, you should also ensure that this right is included in any subsequent agreement that your publisher may make with a third party (e.g. a paperback publisher).

Royalties on sales

Royalties will be calculated as a proportion of the publisher's list price, or of 'net receipts', i.e. the publisher's income. Publishers define 'net receipts' in different ways, so it is wise to ask for an explanation in writing when you are dealing with a new publisher. The rates should normally rise progressively with sales, so that you share in your book's success.

Fees

If you have written the whole book, you should be wary of accepting a fee (however large this may seem) rather than a royalty. If you are a contributor to an edited volume, you cannot normally expect more than a fee.

Advances on royalties

Where an advance is agreed, it is usually divided so that part is payable on signature of the agreement, part on receipt of the typescript, and part on publication (or, to encourage rapid publication, you might stipulate payment of the final part within, say, 10 months of receipt). Whether you are offered an advance, and the size of it, will depend on how well known you are and on the publisher's view of the book's potential. If you have been commissioned to write a book requiring large out-of-pocket expenses (e.g. a travel book), you should certainly expect an advance.

Timing of payments

The contract should be clear about the timing of payments. Royalties are normally paid once a year for educational and academic books, twice a year for fiction and general books. If you live off your royalty income,

18

you should ask for payments to be made twice a year, and for income from the sale of subsidiary rights (see below) to be paid within 60 days of receipt by the publisher providing the advance has been covered. Some publishers are prompter payers than others; the Society of Authors produces a league table.

You should nearly always receive a share of translation, serialization, film, dramatic, broadcasting and extract rights, and of paperback and American rights if they are sold separately. Your share should not be less than 50 per cent and may (particularly for serialization rights) be much higher (up to 90 per cent). There are many ways in which a publisher may be able to make money from your book. If you feel that your contract is not sufficiently comprehensive on the matter of rights income, you should ask for a clause to be inserted along these lines: 'Income from the sale of rights not specified in this agreement shall be shared between the author and the publisher in proportions to be mutually agreed.'

Sale of subsidiary rights

The publisher will normally undertake to publish your book with 'due diligence'. In practice the time it takes to produce a book will vary greatly depending on its complexity; it will often range from 6 to 18 months. If timing is important, you can ask for a particular period to be written into the contract. On the other hand, you should remember that your publisher may need several months to mount a proper international marketing campaign for your book, and insistence on rapid publication could damage its long-term success.

Speed of publication

Your contract is almost bound to include a clause in which you warrant to the publisher that your book contains nothing libellous, defamatory, or indeed anything upon which a third party could reasonably take legal action against you and the publisher. Some publishers (including this one) have insurance arrangements to protect themselves and their authors, but this does

Libel and defamation

19

not give either party a licence to be libellous: legal action usually results in an immediate injunction preventing the sale of the book, with consequent damage to your income and reputation – even if you are innocent. If you suspect that anything you have said might be defamatory or otherwise illegal, you should tell the publisher and may reasonably expect to bear at least half the cost of any legal advice that has to be obtained.

Option clauses

You should in general be wary of giving the publisher an option, that is, the right of first refusal, on your next book (and especially on more than one subsequent book). An option clause, for one book only, may be reasonable, however, if you are an unknown author (particularly a novelist) as the publisher ought to have some share in your future success. You should make sure that such a clause states that the terms of any subsequent agreement between you will be at least as good as those of the present agreement.

Arbitration

Finally, the contract should contain a clause to cover arbitration between you and your publisher should any difference arise between you.

Much more could and has been said about author–publisher contracts. The best book on the subject is *Publishing Agreements*, edited by Charles Clark. Many countries have authors' societies which you can join, either as a published author or when your book has been accepted. Among the benefits you may expect from membership will be advice on contracts.

PART II
Preparing the Typescript and Illustrations

The remainder of this guide is addressed more specifically, though by no means exclusively, to Blackwell
authors. It describes some of the ways in which you can
help us to convert your typescript into a book as quickly
and efficiently as possible. It should not be seen as an
attempt to impose a straitjacket. On the contrary, we
are always happy to accommodate individual authors'
wishes, and to adapt to a book's individual needs. What
follows is a set of recommendations, not a book of
rules. The aim is to provide a convenient source of
reference on many of the questions about physical
presentation, minutiae of style and academic apparatus
that you or your typist may ask.

Please type on one side of A4 paper or its equivalent,
allowing margins of at least an inch on the left and the
right, and using double line-spacing throughout. It is
important to type quotations, notes and bibliographies
double-spaced, as well as the main text, in case any
amendments are required. You should indent the first
line of each paragraph.

**General
presentation**

We need the top copy of the typescript to send to the
typesetter, and a photocopy or corrected carbon to be
used for estimating. Do keep a copy for your own
reference and as an insurance against loss.

A few minor corrections, written clearly above the
line, are quite acceptable, but any addition that includes
names or foreign words is better typed. If a whole paragraph has to be added, type it on a full-size sheet of
paper and indicate clearly where it is to be inserted in the
existing text. Never staple on small pieces of paper as
they can easily go astray.

Pages are best numbered throughout the typescript.
Alternatively, they may be numbered by chapter,
provided the chapter is indicated in the page number
(2/1, 2/2, etc.). A page added late may be numbered,

e.g., 25A, but in that case please make sure that there is a note of warning on the previous page that 25A should follow.

Word-processors

If your typescript has been typed on a word-processor, please attach a list explaining any unusual symbols (e.g. Ø for 0) and eliminate any extraneous symbols (e.g. asterisks denoting that amendments have been made) which might confuse the typesetter. If you have used approximations or codes in early drafts (e.g. 'a for à or [alpha] for α), make sure that the correct accent or symbol is clearly inserted by hand in the final draft.

It may be possible to transfer the text contained on your own floppy disk or magnetic tape (generated by a word-processor or microcomputer) on to the disk used for setting the book. However, this method does require considerable forethought and planning. If you think it may be a good idea in your case, please discuss it with us as early as you can, preferably before you start keying the text at all. Appendix 1 gives more detailed guidance on the preparation of floppy disks for direct setting, and further technical information is available on request.

Pre-delivery checks

It is important that the typescript should be complete. Copy-editing, the first step in the production process, cannot begin until we have the introduction, figures, references, etc. If necessary, an acknowledgements page or a few minor bibliographical details can follow later, but do alert us that they are to come.

The typescript should represent your final thoughts. You will be able to make minor changes (such as updating information) when you check the copy-edited typescript (see the section on copy-editing in part III), but such changes should be kept to a minimum. Proofs should never be regarded as more than an opportunity to check that the typesetter has reproduced the typescript correctly.

The copy-editor will often be able to spot internal

22

discrepancies, but there are a number of details which only the author would notice. Before you deliver your typescript it is a good idea to double-check the exact wording of quotations, bibliographical details, statistics, calculations, dates of events, spellings of names, etc.

Make sure that all author–date references given in the text are duly listed at the end of the typescript; that all abbreviations are explained; that lists of references, abbreviations, glossary, etc., are in alphabetical order.

Please check too that numbering systems used for headings, figures, notes, etc., do not skip or repeat; that notes relate correctly to their indicators in the text; and that cross-references to sections, figures, etc., still apply after revision.

Wherever possible, cross-references should be to chapter or section rather than to page. This saves the cost of inserting a page number at proof. If a page cross-reference is essential, you should either type p. 000, or for your own reference put the typescript page number but cross it through and write 000 above it.

Make sure that there are no phrases which will make the book date too quickly, e.g. 'this year', or which suggest a geographically restricted readership, e.g. 'in this country'. Instead, put the actual date, or name the country. Equally, it is important to remember that terms common in your own discipline may not be so common in related ones. You can often widen the book's market by making sure that special terms are clearly explained.

Headings

Please give chapters arabic numerals and start each on a new page of the typescript. Roman numerals may be used for part or volume numbers.

It is best to restrict the levels of subheading within a chapter to three at the most; normally one or two levels will suffice. Make sure that the different levels are clearly distinguished, either by typing them in different ways, or by writing A in the margin beside the highest level, B beside the next level, etc.

In most books we prefer to avoid numbered sections and subsections within chapters. In print the levels can be more satisfactorily differentiated by using distinct typography. In textbooks, however, numbered headings may serve a useful purpose since cross-reference can then be made to section rather than to page.

Preferred styles

In general we are happy to follow your own preferences on spelling etc. provided you apply a recognized system consistently. If you are in doubt about the best form to use on a point not covered below, please consult the supplementary reading section below. *The Oxford Dictionary for Writers and Editors* is particularly useful.

If you notice an inconsistency or error just before you deliver your typescript, you can simply attach a note indicating which way you would like us to standardize it.

Listed below you will find certain styles which our copy-editors are normally asked to apply. It is very helpful if you can follow them in your typescript. If any are inappropriate for your book, or if you feel strongly against any of them, please let us know.

Spellings

We prefer to use the suffix -ize rather than -ise for words where either spelling is possible. Remember, however, that in 'compromise', 'supervise', etc., the *s* is essential as it is not part of a suffix. In 'analyse' etc. use -yse rather than -yze.

Where French words have been absorbed into English, accents can normally be omitted unless they affect the pronunciation, so: elite, role, regime (unless italicized as in, e.g., *ancien régime*), but café, protégé, cliché.

Write Hicks's, Keynes's, etc., except for classical names, e.g. Socrates'.

We prefer the alternatives: judgement (but judgment in legal works), connection, premise, medieval, focused.

Use single quotation marks normally, reserving double for quoted words within a quotation. In philosophy or linguistics it may be necessary to use single and double quotation marks for different purposes. In that case it is helpful if you can tell us what your system is.

Be consistent in your use of hyphens: do not, e.g., go from 'rate payer', through 'rate-payer', to 'ratepayer'. Avoid dividing on to two lines a word which can be spelt either with or without a hyphen.

If you hyphenate compounds used attributively (e.g. 'twentieth-century history', 'the decision-making process'), please make sure you do it in all such instances. However, the hyphen is not normally needed for predicative use: write 'the best-known man' but 'the man was best known for . . .'. Equally, the hyphen is unnecessary where an unmistakable adverb qualifies an adjective, e.g. 'fully interlocking pieces'.

Where you make a distinction between, e.g., conservative and Conservative, do apply it throughout the typescript.

In general capitals should be used sparingly. It is not necessary to use a capital whenever a title is mentioned, so: the bishop, the local government officer (even when the abbreviated form uses capitals, as in LGO). However, it is best to use a capital in association with a name, so: King John, the Duke of Anjou, etc.

Use lower case for 'south-west' etc., unless it is part of a political unit, so 'northern England' but 'Western Australia'.

Use lower case for 'see figure 2.1', 'see chapter 6', etc.

Underline foreign words to indicate italic, unless they are part of a quotation in a foreign language, or are so common in English that they may be regarded as naturalized. Underline titles of books and journals.

If you want to use italic for other purposes (e.g. to

distinguish use from mention), it is helpful if you tell us what your system is. Italic as a means of emphasis should be avoided as it can be distracting in print.

Abbreviations

Write BBC, TUC, USA, etc., without full stops. MPs, WAAFs, etc., require no apostrophe.

Where the abbreviation is partially or wholly lower case, no full stop is needed if the final letter of the word is used in the abbreviation, so: Mr, St, Ltd, eds, edn, but cf., e.g., i.e., ed., tr.

Units of measurement never require a full stop: km, ha, etc.

A good many abbreviations of Latin words are so familiar that they can be printed in roman rather than italic: ibid., et al., etc.

Try to avoid the use of too many abbreviations in the text: clutches of capitals (LDCs, NGOs, etc.) can be offputting.

It is normally best to use 'for example' and 'that is' in text, reserving e.g. and i.e. for notes.

Dates

Write '16 June 1588' (not June 16th, 1588) or, in a detailed narrative, 'on the 16th'. Write 'the 1930s' (not the 1930's) or, where there is no doubt as to the century, 'the thirties' (not the '30s). Write 'the twentieth century' (not the 20th Cent.).

BC should follow the date; AD should precede it. Periods BC have to be spelt out in full, 330–325 BC. Except in chapter or section headings, dates AD are best abbreviated to 1956–7 or (for a financial or academic year) to 1956/7. Underline c. (for *circa*) to show italic and type the date close up following the full stop.

Other numbers

Adopt a rule that all numbers under 10 (in more technical books) or under 100 (in more literary books) should be spelt out. This rule should not be interpreted too rigidly, so write, e.g., 'between 95 and 101' (not 'between ninety-five and 101'). Never start a sentence with a figure; instead, write it out in full or rephrase the

26

sentence. Use figures for exact measurements attached to units (so 'two girls' but '5 kg') and for cross-references ('see chapter 6'). Percentages are usually given in figures, since this is essential when the percentage contains a fraction (e.g. 6.5 per cent), but in a more general work, where percentages occur infrequently, it may be better to write 'five per cent' etc.

Write 'per cent' in the text; '%' in tables or in notes which cite a number of statistics.

Always write 0.2 etc. (not .2).

Adopt a rule for the treatment of thousands: either 4500 but 45,000; or 4,500 and 45,000; or (in more scientific works) 4000 but 45 000. In tables, of course, the rule may have to be broken to make sure that four- and five-digit numbers line up. Figures in millions are usually better as 'two million' (not 2,000,000), or 2m in more technical works.

Elide numbers as far as possible, so 56–7, 132–4, etc., but make an exception for the teens, so 11–15, 118–19, etc.

Leave a space after p. in page references: p. 60.

Units

Wherever possible, use metric rather than imperial units. In geography, economics, etc., it is important to use SI (Système International, see supplementary reading below) units and abbreviations, so: mm, m, km (but not cm); g (not gm), etc.

Abbreviated units do not change in the plural, so 3 km (not 3 kms).

American spelling and punctuation

In a series or book where some contributors use British spellings and some American, it will normally be necessary to standardize to the forms given above. American spelling and punctuation may, however, be retained if they have been used throughout and/or if the book's market is likely to be predominantly American.

Quotations

Longer quotations (of more than roughly 60 words) should be broken off from the text and set out as 'extracts'. Occasionally shorter passages may be worth treating as extracts, either so that they can be compared with longer passages, or for emphasis, but remember that very short extracts look strange in print.

Please type extracts indented, double-spaced, with an extra space above and below. There is no need to indent the first line of the extract further, even if it begins a new paragraph in the original. Do not insert opening and closing quotation marks, except where they are needed to indicate dialogue within the extract itself.

The original spelling of the quotation should normally be followed exactly (e.g. American or British spellings, -ise or -ize suffixes, etc.). In some books, however, there may be a case for modernizing spelling or silently correcting eccentricities. To determine whether the first letter of a quotation should be a capital or not, you should consistently either follow the original, or standardize according to the way in which the quotation fits into your text.

Where you have omitted words from a quoted passage, either always use three dots, or distinguish consistently between an unfinished sentence (three dots) and a completed sentence (a full stop followed by three dots, i.e. four dots). Any insertions of your own should be enclosed in square brackets. State 'my italics' where appropriate.

Please quote from the same edition of a book throughout your typescript unless there is a special reason not to do so.

If your references are given in notes (see below), place the note indicator after the quotation, whether it is set out as an extract or run on in the text.

If you are using the author–date system (see below), it is often neater to incorporate the reference into the sentence before the extract. Where the reference does follow the extract, it should be in parentheses, following the final full stop of the extract, but without a full stop of its own.

Where a shorter quotation is run on in the text, the reference in parentheses is best typed before the full stop, thus: '. . . in the end' (Smith, 1960, p. 6).

We prefer to punctuate short quotations run on in the text according to the following rules. Where a word or phrase is quoted, the closing quotation mark precedes the full stop. Where a sentence is quoted (i.e. anything with a subject and main verb, whether or not it forms a complete sentence in the original), the full stop precedes the closing quotation mark. In a situation analogous to dialogue, punctuate thus: 'The Pope,' according to Chrimes, 'was responsible.'

Excessive quotation from other works should be avoided. In certain cases, however, it will be essential to quote extensively from a particular source. Please see the section on copyright permissions below for the problems this may raise.

Notes

Substantive, as opposed to reference, notes should be avoided as far as possible. The placing of notes (whether as true footnotes, or at the end of the chapter or book) depends largely on the market and costing of the book. If you have strong feelings about this, do discuss it with us at an early stage.

Whether your notes are to be set as footnotes or as endnotes, they should not be typed at the foot of the page, but at the end of the chapter or at the end of the typescript.

Please number the notes consecutively through each chapter. It is important that there should be no notes called 17a etc. If you need to add a note during revision, please renumber the rest of the notes in the chapter.

Note indicators in the text should be placed at a natural break in the sense and should follow any punctuation except a dash. Please type the indicator above the line, without parentheses.

Do not attach ordinary chapter notes to table headings or figure captions as it may not be possible to place the tables and figures precisely enough to maintain the numbering sequence. Instead, notes and an indication of source should go under a table (see the section on tables below). Explanatory notes about a figure should go in the key and an indication of the source should be incorporated in the caption (see the section on figures and maps below).

Please also avoid attaching note indicators to chapter headings or subheadings as these look strange in print.

Reference systems

The reference system you choose will, of course, largely be dictated by current usage in your own discipline. The styles given below simply express our preferences and will not necessarily be imposed if you have used a consistent, orderly and unambiguous system. The two systems described are, however, widely used and generally preferable to, e.g., numbers referring to an alphabetical list. It is not essential to follow the precise order, use of capitals or punctuation given, but, if you do not, make sure that you apply your own preferred style consistently.

Following the description of the two systems you will find some general points which apply to all reference systems.

Short title

In this system, which is widely used in the humanities, references appear in notes. A full reference is given the first time the work is mentioned in a chapter; further references consist of the author's surname and the title of the work or, if it is long, a shortening of the title. We much prefer to use a short title rather than *op. cit.*, which is less readily recognizable and can be ambiguous.

The system may be used with or without a full bibliography at the end of the book. For most purposes it is enough to include all reference details in the notes. A monograph may sometimes need a bibliography, or a textbook may usefully include one which can serve as a reading list. If you want to include a bibliography as well as notes, it is best to consult your editor at an early stage.

The first reference to a particular work in the notes to any particular chapter should be in the following form.

For books:

C. M. Cipolla, *Before the Industrial Revolution: European society and economy, 1100–1700*, tr. F. Franks (Methuen, London, 1976), p. 60.

John Lynch, *Spain under the Habsburgs*, 2nd edn (2 vols, Basil Blackwell, Oxford, 1981), vol. I: *Empire and Absolutism, 1516–1598*.

For journal articles:

Josiah B. Gould, 'Being, the world and appearance in early Stoicism and some other Greek philosophers', *Review of Metaphysics*, 27 (1974), pp. 261–88, esp. p. 277.

Geoffrey Parkinson, 'I give them money', *New Society*, 5 Feb. 1970.

For articles in edited volumes:

Phyllida Parsloe, 'After-custody: supervision in the community in England, Wales and Scotland', in *Social Work and the Courts*, ed. Howard Parker (Edward Arnold, London, 1979), pp. 16–30, esp. p. 20.

If you have a bibliography, the first reference in the notes can be reduced to author, title, date and page; other publication details will appear in the bibliography.

After the first reference in the chapter, further references consist of the author's surname and the title or, where necessary, a shortening of it:

Cipolla, *Before the Industrial Revolution*, p. 62.
Lynch, *Spain under the Habsburgs*, vol. I, p. 62.
Gould, 'Being, the world and appearance', p. 279.
Parkinson, 'I give them money'.
Parsloe, 'After-custody', p. 22.

If you prefer, further references to articles can use the journal title, or the editor's name, instead of the article title provided this is done consistently. So:

Gould, *Review of Metaphysics* (1974), p. 279.
Parkinson, *New Society*, 5 Feb. 1970.
Parsloe, in Parker (ed.), p. 22.

Where a further reference is to the same work as that given in the immediately preceding note, the only reference required is:

Ibid., p. 25.

In a bibliography the details required are much the same as those given above for first references, but there is less need for parentheses, and the author's surname must come first:

Mieghem, J. von and Oye, P. van (eds), *Biogeography and Ecology in Antarctica*, Junk, The Hague, 1965.

Author–date

This is the most common reference system in the sciences. It largely eliminates the need for notes. Instead, the reference is given in parentheses in a convenient place in the text. It saves a great deal on costs; the disadvantage is that the reader has to turn to the reference list at the end of the book to trace the source, since a date is generally less informative than a short title. Please avoid using any system which combines the disadvantages of the two methods, e.g. using the author–date system but putting the references in notes. There may, however, be a case for creating a note if a long string of references has to be given. A few notes of this type or of the substantive type may be needed even in a book using the author–date system.

The reference in parentheses in the text gives the author's surname and the date of publication. If two or more works by the author have the same date, distinguish them by using a, b, etc. (see below).

Use one of the following forms consistently:

(Barry, 1960a, p. 60; Barnes and Creasey, 1970)

OR   (Barry 1960a: 60; Barnes and Creasey 1970)

Where the author's name is mentioned in the body of the sentence, the reference in parentheses simply consists of the date and, if necessary, the page. For a repeated reference, do not use ibid., but simply repeat the date. If both author and date are clear from the context, a page reference alone, in parentheses, is enough, but please use the form (p. 60), not just (60).

Where two or more references are given together, follow consistently either alphabetical order, or chronological order, or order of importance.

Where authors share a surname it is best to include the initials before the surname throughout so that the reader goes directly to the right part of the reference list.

Use et al. consistently either for books with three or more authors, or for books with four or more authors. All the authors' names should be listed in the reference at the end of the book.

The date given in references in the text should be the date of the edition used. It is sometimes helpful, however, to mention the date of the original edition, or the date of the original of a translation, among the bibliographical details in the reference list.

The list of references should always give the date immediately after the author's name so that the text reference can be traced rapidly. Arrange the references under a particular author's name chronologically; where two or more references have the same date, order them alphabetically by title and designate them a, b, etc. Second and further entries under an author's name can be shown by indentation, as in the examples which follow. Where the whole reference list is quite short, it may be better to repeat the author's name each time for clarity, but this can be wasteful of space in a long list.

For books:

Rotberg, Robert L. and Mazrui, Ali A. (eds) 1970: *Protest and Power in Black Africa*. New York: Oxford University Press.
Sugden, David 1982: *Arctic and Antarctic: a modern geographical synthesis*. Oxford: Basil Blackwell.

For journal articles:

Hull, D. L. 1978a: A matter of individuality. *Philosophy of Science*, 45, 105–60.
1978b: Are species really individuals? *Systematic Zoology*, 23, 80–96.

For articles in edited volumes:

Born, K. E. 1976: Structural changes in German social and economic development at the end of the nineteenth century. In James J. Sheehan (ed.), *Imperial Germany*, New York/London: New Viewpoints, 16–38.

Cannan, Crescy 1975: Welfare rights and wrongs. In R. Bailey and M. Brake (eds), *Radical Social Work*, London: Edward Arnold, 112–28.

*General
points on
references*

Both place and publisher are given in the examples above for the sake of completeness, but it is normally best simply to give the place, or simply to give the publisher. Please ensure, however, that you do not give sometimes one, sometimes the other.

The place should always be a town, not a region or country. In some cases the town alone might be unclear, so it is best to use, e.g., Englewood Cliffs, NJ or Cambridge, Mass. Write Vienna, Munich, etc., rather than Wien, München, etc.

It is important to specify which edition you have used if you give a page number. A reprint is normally identical in pagination, but a new edition or a paperback edition may be reset, in which case the page number may change.

Wherever possible, journal titles should be given in full. In some typescripts abbreviations will be essential in order to save space. If you abbreviate, make sure that the rationale is consistent, and follow official international listings wherever you can. Where an abbreviation takes the form of initials (*JMH, EJ,* BL, EETS, etc.), make sure that italic is used if the abbreviation derives from a journal or a book title, and roman if it derives from a library, series, etc. All abbreviations should be explained.

It is not necessary to give the number as well as the volume of a quarterly journal if the page numbers are cited since almost all such journals are paged by volume. If volume and number are given, please use the form 12, 3 (1974) in the short-title system, or 12 (3) in the author–date system.

34

Any tabular material should be typed on a separate page and assigned a number. Normally tables are best numbered using the chapter number, so the first table in chapter 2 will be table 2.1 etc. If there are few tables, they may simply be called table 1 etc.

In the text there should be a reference to each table by number, e.g. 'see table 2.1' (not 'the following table'). Tables will be placed as near the text reference as possible, but they cannot always appear immediately below the text discussion. If there are only a few tables in your typescript, place each one near its discussion in the text and number the typescript pages continuously to include the tables. If there are many tables, or if they are complicated, it is best to gather them together at the end of the typescript. If you do this, make sure that each table is clearly identified, and add a note in the margin of the relevant page of text saying, e.g., 'Table 2.1 near here'.

The sample table below does not, of course, cover all eventualities but shows how tables should normally be

Table 6.2   Production and costs in selected industries in the United Kingdom, 1978

Industry	Sales (£m)	Cost of materials[a] (% of sales)	Net output (% of sales)	Wages (% of net output)
Chemicals and allied industries	21,542	70.0	30.0	30.4
Food, drink and tobacco	27,482	72.6	27.4	33.8
Metal manufactures	10,419[b]	68.1	31.9	59.7
Mining and quarrying	4,134	26.4	73.6	48.4
Textiles	11,247	58.4	41.6	54.3

[a] Including fuel costs.

[b] The figure represents a marked decline, the causes of which are discussed in detail in chapter 7 below.

Source: Annual Abstract of Statistics, 1981

set out. They should be typed as clearly and consistently as possible, and parallel tables should be laid out in similar ways. The main heading should be explicit but concise. Units should always be stated, either in the main heading, or in parentheses below column headings. Where two levels of column heading are necessary, make sure that it is clear which columns a heading refers to (e.g. by inserting a short horizontal rule). We do not normally print vertical rules in a table: the spacing of the columns should show the meaning sufficiently clearly. Line up all the numbers in a column so that the decimal points are under each other. Please give the source, wherever necessary, below any notes relating to the table.

Lists

Lists should be used sparingly. Where you do list points, make sure that your numbering system is as uniform as possible throughout the typescript. Thus points in major lists could be designated 1 and 2 (without parentheses or a full stop). Points in minor lists (either smaller points or items within a major list) could be designated (a) and (b) (with parentheses, not underlined for italic). Avoid using roman numerals.

If you type each item in the list on a new line, make sure that you follow a consistent layout of indentation and spacing. Follow a consistent rule over the use of a capital or lower-case letter at the beginning of each item and a full stop or semi-colon at the end. You could, e.g., use a capital letter and full stop for sentences, a lower-case letter and semi-colon for words or phrases.

Special symbols and equations

It is helpful if you can make a list of any phonetic, logical, mathematical, etc., symbols required. The best method is to supply a printed list (e.g. of the international phonetic alphabet) and circle the symbols you have used. If a symbol is used infrequently, please indicate which typescript pages it appears on.

It is important that all symbols in the text should be

36

clear and unambiguous. This is often best achieved by writing them neatly by hand rather than devising approximations on the typewriter.

Do make sure that the same conventions for symbols are followed throughout the typescript. Where co-authors are concerned, this will require early consultation.

Foreign alphabets such as Greek, Hebrew and Russian may be difficult to obtain. Please consider carefully whether quotations in the original alphabet are indispensable. If you decide to transliterate instead, do make sure you follow a recognized system consistently.

If bold type is required for vectors, mark $\sim$ under the vector by hand. If bars are required below symbols, please alert us in case they are mistaken for marks indicating italic or bold.

It is usually best not to type underlining to show italic for variables in mathematics. Our copy-editor will mark this by hand. However, if you have strong views on what should be italic and what roman, it is helpful if you let us know. For subscripts we normally use roman for those consisting of the initial letters of the words they represent, but italic for those consisting of mathematical quantities.

Two-tier equations cannot be set as part of an ordinary line of text. Please either convert them into one-line equations by using an oblique stroke, or set them out as displayed equations.

Type all mathematics as clearly as possible, aligning equals signs where necessary. Make sure that you consistently either punctuate displayed equations according to the sense of the surrounding text, or leave them unpunctuated.

An equation number should be enclosed in parentheses and typed at the right-hand margin. Normally equations are best numbered using the chapter number, so the first equation in chapter 2 will be equation 2.1 etc. Text references may be in the form 'see equation (2.1)' or 'see (2.1)'. If there are few numbered equations in the book they may simply be called equation 1 etc.

Figures and maps

Any drawings that are likely to take up more than four or five lines of print should be called figures and assigned numbers.

The figure numbering sequence will usually (but not always) include maps; it may sometimes include photographs as well (see below). Normally figures are best numbered using the chapter number, so the first figure in chapter 2 will be figure 2.1 etc. If there are few figures, they may simply be numbered figure 1 etc.

In the text there should be a reference to each figure by number, e.g. 'see figure 2.1' (not 'see the figure below', or 'see the accompanying diagram', etc.).

Draw the graph, flow-chart, map, diagram, etc., as accurately as you can on a separate piece of paper. We normally employ an artist to do the final drawing for reproduction, but remember that he or she will usually be attempting a faithful replica of your 'rough', not an original interpretation of its content.

Graphs are best drawn on graph paper. Where the precise positioning of curves is important, lists of co-ordinates can be a helpful adjunct to, but not a substitute for, an accurate drawing. Make sure that axes are consistently and explicitly labelled.

Maps should be traced as accurately as possible. Again, an already printed map from which yours is taken can be a helpful addition. A bar scale should appear on every map, either indicating metric units only, or both metric and imperial. Always use SI units and abbreviations. Make sure that figures and maps have explanatory keys where necessary.

It is helpful if you write, e.g., 'Fig. 2.1 near here' in the margin of the typescript. A photocopy of the relevant figure is useful in the typescript (not numbered in with the typescript pages), but the original figure roughs are best gathered together at the end. Please ensure that they are clearly identified.

If you have access to special drawing or cartographic facilities you may want to discuss the possibilities of producing your own artwork. This can be very helpful provided you seek advice in good time on reduction factors, standardization of style, etc. We can supply detailed specifications if, after discussion, you decide to go ahead.

Figure captions should be typed as a separate list, though it is a good idea to include them on the roughs as well for identification. Wherever necessary, the source should be given at the end of the caption. The original source of the figure should always be given, rather than an intermediate work in which the figure has been reproduced from an earlier source. See also the section on copyright permissions below.

Photographs

If it has been agreed that the book should contain photographs and that you are to obtain them, you need to supply good black-and-white prints showing a clear contrast in tonal values. Already 'screened' pictures, such as illustrations from books or magazines, are not normally suitable for reproduction.

Paper clips should never be used on photographs. Either write an identification number (see below) lightly on the back, or affix a small self-adhesive label. Identify the top of the picture wherever there might be confusion. If part of it may be (or should be) omitted, please show this on an overlay or on an accompanying photocopy.

In highly illustrated books it is helpful if you can suggest ideal relative sizes for reproducing the photographs. This can be done by writing A (large), B (medium), or C (small) lightly on the back. The choice will depend both on the quality of the original print and on the importance of the subject to your discussion.

When you send in your typescript and photographs, please include a complete list of captions. Since the production department and the copy-editor may need to be working with the illustrative material simultaneously, it is helpful if you can also send a set of photocopies of the photographs and a duplicate list of captions.

The caption may include a note of the source of the illustration. Alternatively, all the sources may be collected together in a separate acknowledgements list at the beginning or end of the typescript. See also the section on copyright permissions below.

If you frequently refer to the illustrations in the text (particularly if you refer to illustrations in another section or chapter), you will need to assign consecutive numbers to them. The photographs may be numbered in a continuous sequence through the book. Alternatively, photographs may be included with diagrams, graphs, etc., in the sequence of figures and numbered by chapter (see the section on figures above). If, however, text-references to photographs are unnecessary, it is often simpler not to number them at all. This allows greater freedom in the ordering of photographs and also makes it possible to slip in a late arrival or omit a non-arrival.

Numbers are helpful for identification purposes even when they are not to be used in the final book. (If they are not be be printed, then the numbers do not have to be kept consecutive.) Please write the identification number in the margin of the most relevant discussion in the typescript. We shall not always be able to position the photograph precisely but we need to know the ideal placing. A circled note of the relevant typescript page number is also helpful in the margin of the list of captions.

If it has been agreed that our picture researcher will obtain the original photographs, you should provide as full a briefing as you possibly can. If you know exactly what you want, then supply a photocopy and full details of the whereabouts of the original. If you simply want, say, a medieval cathedral, then outline the purpose of the illustration, whether it should be an interior or exterior, etc.

Copyright permissions

Your contract will tell you whether it is your responsibility or ours to obtain, and to pay for, permission to use photographs, figures, long quotations, etc. If the responsibility is yours, you should write to the copyright holder before you send in your final typescript since the process can often take a considerable time.

Different countries have different rules, but in the UK copyright subsists for fifty years after the author's death or, if the work was not published during his or her lifetime, fifty years after first publication. Unpublished work remains permanently in copyright.

It is always essential to acknowledge the source of a photograph, figure, quotation, etc., whether or not you need to apply for permission to reproduce it.

For photographs, permission is almost always required. If the photograph is of a painting or drawing, the artist (or his or her heirs) and art gallery, as well as the photographer or photographic agency, will normally have to give permission.

It is prudent also to apply for permission to reproduce all maps, plans, figures, etc.

With the exception of the cases discussed in the next paragraph, it is necessary to apply for permission to quote a 'substantial part' of a written work. This applies to situations such as quoting someone's description of a place, using a quotation to back up an opinion you are voicing, etc. Here, 'substantial' really means important rather than large, but it is often taken to imply anything more than a line or two of poetry, or about 100 words of prose.

If you are quoting 'for purposes of criticism or review', or if you are reporting on current events, the 'fair dealing' rule enables you to quote more freely. A rough guideline might be up to a quarter of a poem, or a single prose extract of up to 400 words, or a series of extracts from the same work of up to 800 words.

It should be emphasized that the Copyright Act (1956) gives no indication of the number of words that can be quoted; these guidelines merely reflect fairly widespread practice. They are often held to be over-cautious and application for permission is frequently more of a courtesy than an obligation.

For a book of readings or reprinted articles, it is always necessary to apply for permission. There is an exception relating to 'anthologies intended for use in schools', but this cannot be invoked for books at university level.

You should normally apply to the publisher or the journal in the first instance. The sample letter below shows some of the details which should be included. If you are unsure whether your book is to be published in paperback as well as hardback, or whether it is likely to have a market in the USA, do consult your editor. Acquiring American rights can often double the cost, so it is sensible to check whether you need 'world rights' or 'world rights excluding the USA'. If you find that some publishers quote much higher fees than others, it is well worth letting them know that their charges are above the average and asking them to reconsider.

```
Permissions Department                          10 London Rd
Smith and Hall Ltd                                   Oxford


                                             6 January 1985

Dear Sir or Madam,

I am at present writing a book entitled  Great Literature of the
World which is to be published by Basil Blackwell in hardback
and paperback editions in the Spring of 1986.  I should be very
grateful for permission to include in it approximately 500 words
from your publication:

        C. Forester, Village Life, 1969, pp. 6-7.

I attach a photocopy of the extract concerned.

I require non-exclusive world rights.  If it is necessary to
apply separately for American rights, please let me know the
name and address of the American publisher.

My book is intended as a student textbook [or a scholarly text
of limited circulation etc.], so it is important to keep the
costs down as far as possible.  I hope that you will bear this
in mind in setting the fee, if any.

I shall, of course, include an acknowledgement of the source.
Please let me know if you have any special requirements as to
the form this should take.

Yours faithfully,



Bernard Constance
```

Series If your book is to appear in a series, it is a good idea to look at one or two recent volumes. We do redesign series from time to time, and particular volumes may

42

have special requirements, but in general styles applied to previous books are likely to be applied to yours.

Do make sure that you consult us or the series editor well in advance over the readership level, the general aims of the series, the style for references and notes, whether lists of further reading are wanted, etc.

Volume editors should, wherever possible, issue precise instructions on coverage, readership level, reference system to be used, levels of subheading, style and symbol conventions, etc., well in advance of the deadline by which the final drafts of contributions are expected.

Edited volumes

It is important that any major editorial changes by the volume editor should be cleared with the contributors before the final typescript is delivered. It is not always possible to send the copy-edited typescript to contributors for checking, and changes in proof are very expensive. If the volume has been in preparation for a long time, it is a good idea to ask contributors, shortly before delivery to us, whether they have any additions or changes to make.

It is quite often necessary, for reasons of speed and efficiency, to ask volume editors to be entirely responsible for the proofreading. In this case it is, of course, still more important that contributors should have approved all changes at typescript stage, and that they should be fully aware that they will not see proofs.

Sometimes we may have asked you as volume editor to integrate the contributors' separate references into a unified list for the whole book. In this case, please resolve any discrepancies that arise before you deliver the typescript, e.g. conflicting dates for the same work, reference to a paperback edition in one contribution and a hardback in another, etc. Often it is only when the integrated list is ready that problems emerge such as references to two different works by the same author in the same year which need to be distinguished as a and b. It is important, therefore, when you have finished the list, to go back through the text adding the a or b as relevant in such instances.

Translations   Translators should impose consistency of style and presentation, etc., as discussed elsewhere in this guide. Any irregularities of numbering system, list layout, etc., in the original edition should be put right.

Please standardize the reference style where necessary rather than reproducing an inconsistent original. It is very helpful if you can add queries about missing bibliographical details, page references, etc., to any queries on meaning and content you send to the author.

In books directed at a student readership it is normally best to quote from English translations of works rather than from the originals. If you do so, please use the exact words of a published translation, and give a reference to the translation in place of the author's original reference. Where no published translation exists, it may still be justifiable to translate the extract, but in that case the original reference should be retained. If you are in doubt about such matters, do consult us.

Look out particularly for quotations from English books or from translations of English books. If your author has given his or her own translation, or quoted in his or her own language from a published translation, do not retranslate into English, but look up the original in a library and quote it exactly, giving the English reference only.

New editions   It is sometimes possible to use a good deal of the original setting in a new edition; sometimes it will be more economical to reset the whole text. Do discuss with us in good time which method is likely to be most appropriate for your book.

If much of the original setting is to be used, you can mark minor changes in a copy of the book and attach a typescript of new material. Make sure that there can be no doubt where new material is to be inserted.

If the book is to be reset, please either produce an entirely new typescript, or one consisting partly of new material and partly of pages photocopied or cut from the book.

Check carefully for cross-references which may need to change.

44

PART III

Copy-editing, Proofs and Index

When you have delivered your final typescript to your editor, he or she will pass it on to a desk editor. At Basil Blackwell desk editors are responsible for seeing books through their copy-editing and proofing stages. The actual copy-editing will normally be done by a free-lancer under the desk editor's guidance. The copy-editor's task is to read carefully through the typescript to make sure that everything is clear, both for the eventual reader and for the typesetter.

A good many queries may arise from this. If time and distance allow, the typescript will be returned to you with the queries so that you may check on the work done. It is much more economical to change anything at this stage than it ever will be again, so this is also your opportunity to add any finishing touches.

Copy-editing

Once you have checked the copy-edited typescript, it will be sent for typesetting. The desk editor will discuss the proofing schedule with you as soon as dates are known. It is very important to keep to the schedule as closely as you possibly can. Do let us know in good time if you have travel plans over the relevant period.

The proofs sent to you will normally already have been made up into pages and numbered. So, unless you find major problems (e.g. the omission or repetition of large portions, the misplacing of figures, etc.), it should be possible to compile the index (see below) at the same time as reading your proofs.

You will receive two sets of proofs, the 'marked set' on which you should show the corrections, and a spare set for you to keep. The copy-edited typescript will also be enclosed to enable you to check the proofs in detail. It is important to return the typescript with the marked set of proofs. However, if you would like it back eventually, do let the desk editor know.

Please show corrections on the marked set of proofs as clearly and concisely as possible. The proof-correction marks listed overleaf should help you to do this.

Proofs

		In text	**In margin**
To substitute		make	*d*
	OR	they tend letters	*give*
To transpose		list	*list*
	OR	to boldly go	⌐⌐
To delete		purse	⌢
	OR	he also cared tod	⌢
To insert		tiht	*gh*
	OR	they gone	*had*
To close up		over reach	⌢
To insert space		self knowledge	Y
To change to italic		self knowledge	⌐⌐
To change italic to upright type		self knowledge	⊬
To change to bold		the vector r	∿
To change capital to lower case		the State	≢
To change lower case to capital		the state	≡
To start a new paragraph		ends here. In the next	⌐
	OR	the discussion ends here. In the next lecture Johns	⌐

	In text	In margin
To run on	ends here.⤵ In the next lecture	⟲⟶
OR	the discussion ends here. ⟵In the next lecture	⟍
To insert space between lines	⟩the discussion ends here. ⟋In the next lecture Johns	
To close up space between lines	the cavalry ⟮the paratroops the gunners	
To substitute or insert note indicator or superior	According to Johns⋀this	²⟋
To substitute or insert inferior	the formula H⟋O is	⟋₂
To stet (if you make a mistake and want to restore the original)	the ~~saints~~ were important	~~bishops~~ ⊘

To make punctuation changes:

Text mark / to substitute OR ⋀ to insert

Margin mark	⊙	⊡	;	,	❞❞	( )	⊢⊣	⊢⊣	⊘
	full stop	colon	semi- colon	comma	quotation marks	paren- theses	hyphen	dash	oblique stroke

Put / after each correction that does not already end in a caret (omission sign). This is especially important when two or more correction marks are required on one line.

Example: *d*/ ⊙/ ≡/

Extracts from BS 5261: Part 2: 1976 are reproduced by permission of the British Standards Institution. Complete copies of the document can be obtained from BSI at Linford Wood, Milton Keynes MK14 6LE.

It is important to use different colours when marking your proofs, so that the typesetter can allocate costs fairly:

The typesetter may already have used **green** or **black** to note his or her errors.

Use **red** to show further typesetting errors (i.e. anywhere that the typesetter has departed from the copy-edited typescript).

Use **blue** to show your own essential changes, but do please keep these to an absolute minimum.

If you think it is necessary to distinguish your own changes from publisher's errors (e.g. copy-editing mistakes), use **black** (if not already appropriated by the typesetter) or **pencil** for publisher's errors. Never mark these in red as the typesetter cannot be expected to correct them free of charge.

Making amendments at proof stage is dispro-portionately expensive. If there is a major problem, please ring the desk editor before spending time mark-ing extensive changes on the proofs. Your contract will normally state that author's corrections exceeding 10 per cent of the setting cost will be deducted from royalties. Remember that the initial setting of a page is much more straightforward and automated than correc-tion, which is fiddly and mostly done by hand.

Where you have to make a change, substitute material of the same length as that set wherever possible. It is just as difficult to omit as to add at page-proof stage. Any change that entails moving material from one page to another may also throw out the index.

Make sure that you insert on the proofs the answers to any queries left over from the copy-editing stage. The typesetter may also raise queries, either on the proofs or on the typescript. Please answer these clearly. If any query seems to be directed more at the publisher than at the author, do draw the desk editor's attention to it when you return your proofs.

It is your responsibility to insert page numbers in place of 'see p. 000' etc. for cross-references. This can be done at page-proof stage unless there are major problems. Please also make sure that you insert page numbers on the table of contents, list of illustrations, etc. If page numbers have already been inserted by the typesetter, do check that they are accurate.

Remember to check headings, captions, page numbering, consistency of layout, etc., as well as the actual words of the text.

Please read your proofs with the greatest possible care as we cannot normally undertake a separate full-scale proofreading. It is very helpful if you can, when you return the proofs, list any pages the desk editor should look at (e.g. where material may have to move from one page to another, whether because of typesetting errors or your own changes).

Indexing

Your contract will tell you whether the preparation of the index is your responsibility or the publisher's. The author is often his or her best indexer, starting from the vantage point of a thorough knowledge of the purposes of the book and its potential readership. However, if you prefer, the desk editor can arrange for a professional indexer to do the work. (If the index is your responsibility, then the cost of this will be deducted from future royalties.)

It is sensible to do the bulk of the work on your index when you receive the page proofs: converting typescript page numbers into printed page numbers takes time and can be hazardous. However, it is certainly a good idea to think carefully about the structure of the index well in advance. *Book Indexing* by M. D. Anderson is an invaluable short guide to methods; copies can be borrowed from the desk editor on request.

One integrated index is generally preferable to separate ones for subjects and authors. Restrict yourself, as far as possible, to main entries and sub-entries (avoiding sub-sub-entries).

The heading to a main entry should normally be a

noun (with or without an adjective preceding it), not an adjective on its own, nor a verb. Use a concrete, specific term in preference to a vague, general one. Where there are two or more possible synonyms, use the one the reader is most likely to look up and put all the relevant page numbers under that entry; do not put half the page numbers under one synonym and half under the other. If the two words are closely related but are not synonyms, put the relevant references under each, adding a cross-reference to the other.

Do not index passing mentions which give no information about the topic or person. There is no need to index the foreword or preface unless it gives pertinent information not found elsewhere in the book. Notes should be indexed only if they give additional information about a topic or person not mentioned in the text itself. References in notes or author–date references in parentheses in the text do not necessarily have to be indexed: names appearing in the index are often best restricted to people whose work is discussed in detail. Bibliographies and reference lists never need to be indexed.

The index should be typed double-spaced on A4 paper, in a single column, although it will normally be set in two columns. Please use one of the following layouts for the main entries and sub-entries:

constitutional reform, 2, 4, 10, 102, 112–18,
    166–8, 200
  in Britain, 12, 14, 62–8, 85–93, 156–63,
    210
  in France, 70–80
  see also Reform Acts

OR

constitutional reform, 2, 4, 10, 102, 112–18,
    166–8, 200; in Britain, 12, 14, 62–8, 85–93,
    156–63, 210; in France, 70–80; *see also* Reform
    Acts

The choice between these two different layouts will depend upon the length of your main entries and the number of pages available for the index. The second method saves a good deal of space; in very complicated indexes, the first layout may be clearer.

The following very rough guide on length may be helpful. One column of a double-column index will on average have 50 lines of about 30 characters each in print. So a printed page might accommodate around 75 entries (main entries and sub-entries). The number of pages available cannot be known until proofs are ready, but a 250-page book might be expected to have an index of 6 to 8 pages. Do contact the desk editor when your proofs arrive if you need advice on the space available.

The wording and punctuation of entries in your index should be consistent and minimal. Make sure that you use the same spelling, hyphenation, etc., as in the text. Type the first letter of each entry lower case, unless the word is a proper name.

Sub-entries are usually best listed in alphabetical order ignoring such words as 'and', 'at', 'in', 'of', etc. So:

recreational facilities
   for disabled, 15, 27
   in parks, 110–15
   and rates, 226–35

Recheck the alphabetical order both of main entries and of sub-entries on your index cards or slips before you start typing the index. Mc, M' and Mac are best ordered as though they were all spelt Mac. Leave an extra space between the As and the Bs, the Bs and the Cs, etc.

Avoid using 'ff'. It is much better to give the last page number of the discussion as well as the first. Never use a chapter number instead of page numbers.

Distinguish between, e.g., 65, 66 for separate short references and 65–6 for a continuous discussion. Elide most numbers fully to 135–7 etc. but, for the teens, retain two figures thus: 11–16, 115–19.

Supplementary reading

To find publishers' and agents' addresses and interests:

Writers' and Artists' Yearbook, A. & C. Black, published annually.
Literary Market Place: The Directory of American Book Publishing, R. R. Bowker Co., published annually.

On contracts:

Clark, Charles (ed.), *Publishing Agreements*, 2nd edn, Allen & Unwin, 1984.

To resolve spelling problems:

The Oxford Dictionary for Writers and Editors, Clarendon Press, 1981.

Three useful pamphlets in the Cambridge Authors' and Publishers' Guides series:

Butcher, Judith, *Typescripts, Proofs and Indexes*, Cambridge University Press, 1980.
Anderson, M.D., *Book Indexing*, Cambridge University Press, 1971.
Scarles, Christopher, *Copyright*, Cambridge University Press, 1980.

A further guide to copyright:

Gibbs-Smith, C. H., *Copyright Law concerning Works of Art, Photographs and the Written and Spoken Word* (Museums Association Information Sheet 7), 3rd edn, Museums Association, 1978.

General style guides:

Hart's Rules for Compositors and Readers, 39th edn, Oxford University Press, 1983.
MHRA Style Book, 3rd edn, Modern Humanities Research Association, 1981.

For Système International units:

Quantities, Units and Symbols, 2nd edn, Royal Society, 1975, with addenda, 1981.

Providing your text on a floppy disk

If it has been agreed that you should supply your text on a floppy disk or magnetic tape, please send in the following sample material at an early stage: a list of the 'interface codes' you propose to use (see below), a disk or magnetic tape, together with matching printed-out 'hard copy', containing a file of all the characters on your keyboard (from top left to bottom right, first in normal mode, then in shift, then in supershift, if you have it) and a sample section. This will enable us to advise you about problems and suggest improvements before the keying operation has progressed too far.

Certain basic codes can be helpful but a welter of codes can make copy-editing difficult: it is important to achieve a balance. Codes are certainly useful for different levels of heading, different kinds of text (such as lists or extracts), to indicate italic type, superscript for note numbers, etc. Please make sure that you apply the codes you decide upon consistently, and that you do not forget to use the code for ending the heading, extract, etc., as well as for beginning it. If you want advice on suitable codings, please contact us direct.

When your text is in its final form, you should deliver two sets of 'hard copy', together with the file of characters on your keyboard, and the list explaining the codes used. Please tell us the total character count as well if your machine has recorded it. Do point out any special problems such as the fact that square brackets, asterisks, etc., have been used for coding but are also needed in their own right on specific pages. Do make sure that the hard copy reflects precisely what is on the disk; never use correcting fluid on the hard copy.

The text will be copy-edited in the usual way and returned to you. In addition to dealing with queries, you may also be asked to key in all the changes marked by the copy-editor (provided you find them acceptable). If the changes are extensive you will be asked to provide fresh hard copy with the final floppy disk, in addition to returning the original hard copy marked by the copy-editor.

The typesetter will then transfer the text on to the setting disk, insert instructions on layout and typefaces, and produce page proofs. You will need to check these carefully, even though the basic material should appear exactly as originally keyed. You will also need to insert any page cross-references and compile the index in the normal way.

In keying your text, please use double line-spacing throughout (even for extracts and notes). Do not leave extra space between paragraphs. The beginning of a paragraph may be shown by indenting a standard number of spaces, preferably five. Alternatively, a code may be used.

Please be particularly careful to follow the preferred styles outlined in this guide (single quotation marks, -ize spellings, USA without full stops, etc.) to avoid extensive changes after copy-editing.

Accuracy and consistency are, of course, more than usually important. Make sure you always leave a single space between words; do not justify lines even if your machine has this capability. Please leave only one space after all forms of punctuation (including a full stop). In abbreviations such as 'e.g.' no additional space is required in the middle, but a space should be left in 'p. 60' and similar references, and between initials, e.g. A. B. Smith. A note number (coded for superscript) should follow immediately after the punctuation mark.

It is safest never to divide words at the end of the line as an unwanted hyphen could be retained when the text is rerun through the setting machine. Please be consistent in the way you represent a dash. If your machine does not have a special symbol, it is best to use a hyphen with a space before and after it. If you want to indicate an 'en rule' rather than a hyphen for, e.g., rural–urban conflicts, use a double hyphen without any space before or after it. An en rule is also used in print between numbers but this can be specified automatically.

Opening and closing quotation marks are different in most printed typefaces but identical on word-processors and microcomputers. It is helpful if you can differentiate, e.g. by using an asterisk (or some such symbol) to show an opening single quotation mark (two asterisks can be used for double), reserving the normal sign for a closing quotation mark or an apostrophe. In print a prime (a') is also different from a quotation mark and so may require a special code.

Please make sure that all symbols are carefully distinguished, e.g. lower case l, arabic numeral 1 and roman numeral I, capital O and 0 for zero.

It is best not to indent material such as extracts or lists but to use a code instead. Leave a consistent space above and below extracts or lists. Equations or set-out examples should be indented a different number of spaces from the ordinary paragraph indent.

Complicated equations and tables may be reset by the typesetter and will certainly have to be checked individually for layout as they are transferred to the setting machine. Complications of this kind are one of the major factors in deciding whether a book can be set using the author's disk, so do discuss the problems with us in good time.

Tables should be typed on separate pages and gathered together at the end of the typescript. Figures should be presented in the normal way but it is helpful to have captions and keys on disk. You can indicate the placing of tables and figures either by a code in the text or in red pen in the margin of the hard copy.

Notes should normally be typed together at the end of the book or at the end of the chapter. Please do not indent continuation lines or leave extra space between notes. If it has definitely been agreed that notes will be set at the foot of the page, you may be asked to intersperse them in the text, typing the notes immediately following the paragraph in which they are referred to. This is only helpful if we are using automatic page make-up equipment, so please ask before setting your notes out this way.

A reference list is best typed with indented continuation lines so that there is no confusion about where an entry ends.